MW00387750

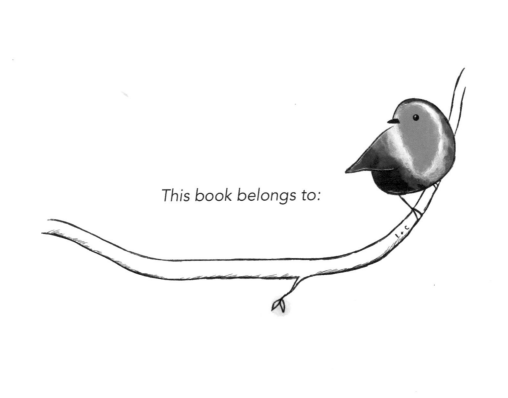

This book belongs to:

A Gentle Introduction to OpenSearch
Written and illustrated by Mitch Seymour

Story direction by Nick Knize and Praveen Sameneni
Art direction by Elyse Seymour
Edited by Nathan Bower

First printing, 2023.

Round Robin Publishing
www.roundrobin.pub
 ✉ hello@roundrobin.pub

A Gentle Introduction to OpenSearch

Written and illustrated by Mitch Seymour

for Chloe & Izzy

When the kits were very small, mealtime was easy. The girls only wanted one or two kinds of food, so everything fit nicely into the Fox family's cupboard.

Searching the cupboard was simple too. There wasn't much to look through, and the kits only knew a few words, like "milk" and "bananas", so searching for a specific meal took no time at all.

As the kits grew older, something changed. They not only ate more food, but also more kinds of food. The cupboard became crowded, which made it difficult for the foxes to find anything.

2 WEEKS   6 WEEKS   3 MONTHS

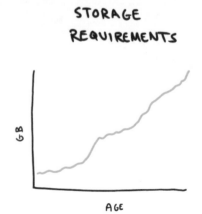

STORAGE REQUIREMENTS

Being small animals of Very Little Patience, the kits would cry if their parents couldn't find ingredients quickly enough. So, the fox parents worked very hard to find and prepare meals as quickly as possible.

One day, the Fox family invited their Friends and Relations over. After seeing their struggles during mealtime, one of their relations had a plan. The Fox family would build some shelves to make searching easier.

Using wood from some old **tables**, they created a series of shelves for storing the ingredients neatly into **rows** and **columns**.

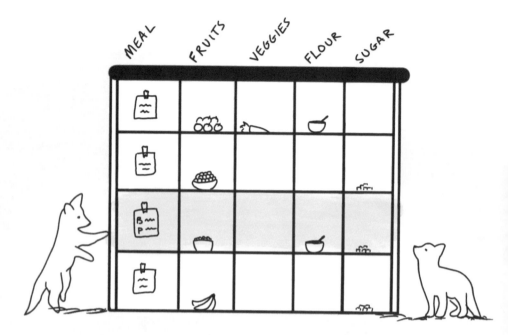

The idea was simple. Each **row** would contain the ingredients for a single meal, and each **column** would contain a single type of ingredient.

So if the kits wanted blueberry pancakes, the parents simply needed to find the correct row.

The foxes could also quickly find meals with certain ingredients. For example, if the kits wanted something with mango, the parents could quickly search the *fruits* column. This is called **structured search**.

The foxes were very proud of their new storage system, which they called **relational storage**, after their Relation who suggested it. Relational storage worked well for a medium amount of storage and precise searches.

RELATIONAL
- HIGHLY ORGANIZED
- ROWS + COLUMNS
- STRUCTURED SEARCH
- EXAMPLES:
  - POSTGRES
  - MYSQL
  - AURORA

But as the kits grew older, they no longer wanted to eat from a fixed menu. They wanted to mix and match ingredients freely, and their meals became **less structured**.

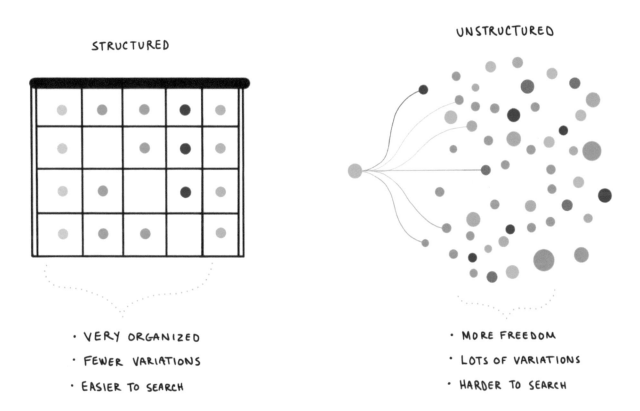

STRUCTURED

UNSTRUCTURED

- VERY ORGANIZED
- FEWER VARIATIONS
- EASIER TO SEARCH

- MORE FREEDOM
- LOTS OF VARIATIONS
- HARDER TO SEARCH

The relational system, which only had so much space and needed every meal to be organized similarly, became harder to use. The foxes had to keep adding new columns (which took a lot of planning), and the new ingredients caused the cupboard to overflow.

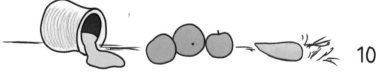

Searching became difficult too as the kits learned new words. Instead of asking for something specific, like "lemon pie", they would describe what they were hungry for (for example, "something rich and sour").

This meant the parents could no longer quickly search the columns. Instead, they had to search each shelf.

Searching one shelf at a time is called a **full table scan**, and it can take a lot of time.

SEARCH VOCABULARY

BEFORE   AFTER   PROJECTION

COLD + RICH

ITALIAN

FANCY

SOUR

LIGHT + FRESH

One day, while half-watching the news and half-thinking of breakfast, Dad Fox heard about a new **data warehouse** being built down the street. The announcer said it would be huge, with shelves and columns as far as the eye could see!

DATA WAREHOUSE

- ENORMOUS SPACE
- ROWS & COLUMNS
- HIGH VOLUME, SLOWER SEARCH

EXAMPLE: REDSHIFT

It sounded like a giant cupboard, which would let the foxes store more food.

But warehouses are busy places, and they are designed for moving and storing enormous amounts of items.

They're not great at finding a single meal very quickly whenever a tummy rumbles, and their columns would put *too much structure* around the kits' meals.

As the foxes continued their search for a solution, they learned about many different storage systems from their friends in the forest.

On one hand, the Otter family stored everything in fast-moving **streams** because they wanted to eat meals continuously and in a particular order. These hungry and picky eaters were very fun to watch!

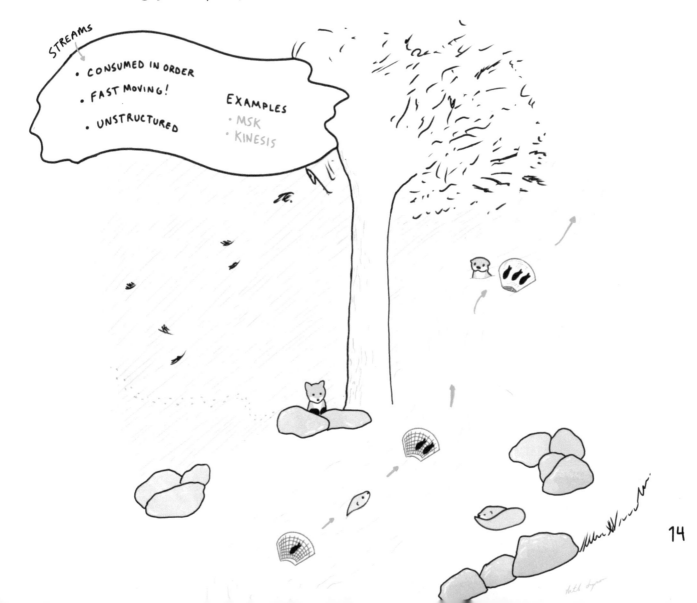

STREAMS
- CONSUMED IN ORDER
- FAST MOVING!
- UNSTRUCTURED

EXAMPLES
- MSK
- KINESIS

On the other hand, the Duck family next door used a **data lake**, which was less structured and could hold nearly *any type of ingredient* (which the ducks placed in **buckets).**

Their lake was really big, and the ducks never tired of eating. But searching a lake would still take far too long.

DATA LAKES

- SEEMINGLY INFINITE
- UNSTRUCTURED
- OBJECTS IN BUCKETS
- EXAMPLE: S3

BUCKET

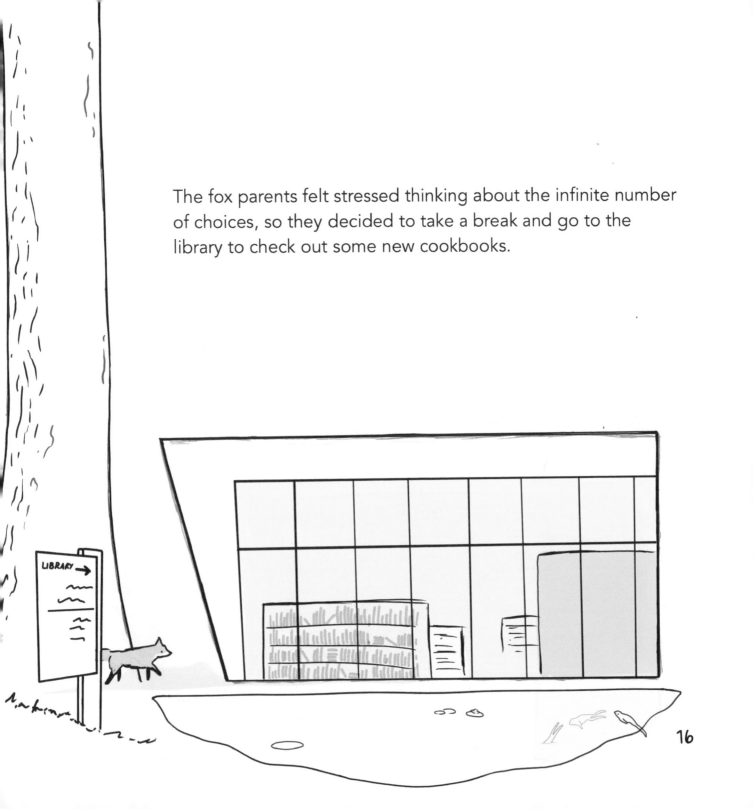

The fox parents felt stressed thinking about the infinite number of choices, so they decided to take a break and go to the library to check out some new cookbooks.

LIBRARY →

16

At the end of one of the cookbooks, Mom Fox came to an **index**, which listed the most important words in the book and also the pages where they could be found.

This index seemed very useful for finding things.

By listing the location of each ingredient, or **term**, in the book, searching for recipes was very fast and even fun! So she asked herself, "Could we use an index like this to quickly find other things, like food for our kits?"

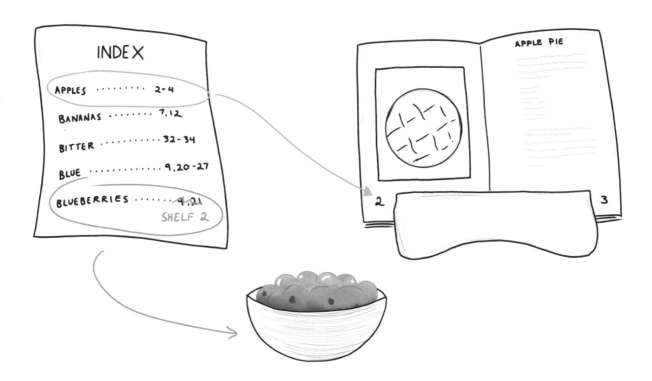

The fox parents went home and eagerly waited for their kits to fall asleep. After the sun went down, they got to work.

As Dad Fox pulled each ingredient down from the shelves, Mom Fox noted the types, colors, and flavors of each ingredient, as well as any other information they might want to search for in the future.

She was going to use these descriptions to build her own list of terms, just like the index in the cookbook!

However, before writing the words down, she needed to take a few steps to make searching easier. She called these steps **analyzers** because she needed to look closely at each term and prepare them for future searches.

There were several steps to take, but they could be chained together, one after the other. And, with some help from her friend, Small, she learned how to string them together to create an **analyzer chain**.

First, Mom Fox split complicated phrases, like "bananas and cream", into smaller parts, called **tokens**. For example, "bananas and cream" became three tokens: **bananas, and, cream** (one for each word).

Small thought this was a very interesting idea. She always knew that little things were very important, so she eagerly helped break up the big phrases.

ANALYZERS   STEP 1

GET TOKENS

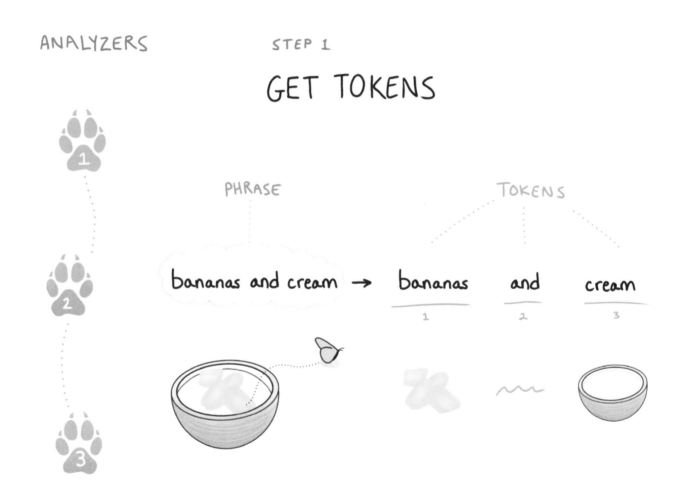

Then, Mom Fox removed any words that didn't seem important. For example, in the phrase "bananas and cream", the word "**and**" isn't very useful for searching, so she didn't bother keeping it.

She called the unimportant words **stop words** and threw them away to keep the index from getting too cluttered.

ANALYZERS

STEP 2

REMOVE STOP WORDS

- BANANAS AND CREAM

- JAM ON TOAST

- PANCAKES WITH SYRUP

- EGG IN A HOLE

- FRUITS OF THE FOREST

Finally, she learned that she could group related ingredient names, like "bananas" and "banana", by analyzing each word and removing any extra word endings.

For example, she could search for "bananas and cream" and "banana bread" using the word "banana" as long as she removed the extra "s" from "bananas". Removing extra letters is called **stemming**, and it makes searching a lot easier!

ANALYZERS

STEP 3

STEMMING

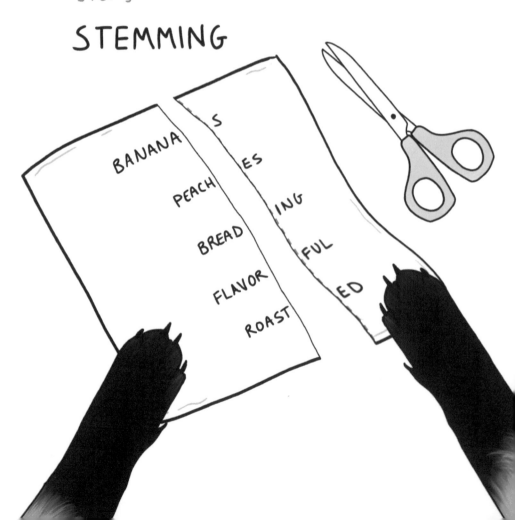

Once Mom Fox was happy with her list of terms, she asked Dad Fox where he would put each ingredient. Since he no longer had to stick to the cupboard, he put them all over the house.

Normally, Dad Fox got in trouble for leaving his things all over the house. This time, it was okay. He put the fruit in the den, the herbs in the kitchen, and the honey in the cellar.

MUDROOM

INGLENOOK

BEDROOMS

WELCOME

DEN

DISTRIBUTED STORAGE

CELLAR

24

Finally, Mom Fox wrote down the location of each ingredient in her notebook, which she called an **inverted index**.

"Inverted" just means that she could search for ingredients in the opposite direction as before.

This was like the little fox she always sees at the edge of the lake, who wants to do the same things as her but in an Opposite Sort of Way.

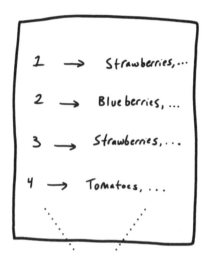

1 → Strawberries,···

2 → Blueberries, ...

3 → Strawberries, ...

4 → Tomatoes, ...

Blueberries → 2

Strawberries → 1,3

Tomatoes → 4

INVERTED

25

The following day, it was time to test out the new system. When the little kits woke up, the littlest one wanted something **sweet** and **dreamy** for breakfast.

Mom Fox searched for the terms in her index and learned that Dad Fox had placed some **strawberry dream cake** in the den. In no time at all, their bellies were filled with dream cake and the kits played happily on the floor.

STRAWBERRY
DREAM CAKE

• CAKE → 8,9-10

• CARROT → 10,15

• CEVICHE → 22

• CHEESE → 24-28,31

• COCONUT → 19

• DAIRY → 2-14, 30

• DARK → 23,27

• DILL → 17

• DONUT → 28

• DREAM → 9 (DEN)

26

The system worked and the foxes were very happy! From now on, whenever they needed to find a meal or ingredient, they simply *Opened* the index and *Searched* for the proper terms.

They called their system **OpenSearch**, and shared it with everyone in the forest.

OpenSearch.org

Printed in the USA
CPSIA information can be obtained
at www.ICGtesting.com
LVHW072308201023
761654LV00007B/163